A Time for Everything

The Kevin Zimmerman Story
Second Edition

A Time for Everything

The Kevin Zimmerman Story
Second Edition

Michael L. White

Parson Place Press
Mobile, Alabama

*A Time for Everything: The Kevin Zimmerman
Story, Second Edition* by Michael L. White
Copyright © 2008 and 2012 by Kevin Zimmerman.
All rights reserved.

Cover Design by Just Ink

ISBN 13: 978-0-9842163-6-9

Library of Congress Control Number: 2011941098

Dedication

To American military service members serving faithfully all around the globe: thank you for helping to preserve our way of life, for the privilege of sleeping in peace, and the most blessed benefit of all – for taking our place in battle.

NOTE: As one way of showing our gratitude, a portion of the proceeds from the sale of this book will go to support organizations that serve wounded American veterans, deployed soldiers and their families.

Contents

Acknowledgements

First and foremost, I want to thank God for giving me this assignment, and I do believe God did assign it to me. It started out simply enough, but completing the first edition took far longer than I expected or intended, and God would not let me let it go until I finished it. It seems to me now to have been a little like Jacob wrestling with the Angel of the Lord, except it was actually *God* Who would not let *me* go until I blessed *Him*!

Lest you think me sacrilegious for saying that, remember the psalm of David, where he said, "Bless the Lord, O my soul: and all that is within me, bless his holy name. Bless the Lord, O my soul, and forget not all his benefits" (Psalm 103:1, 2 KJV). I believe God wanted me to bless Him in the writing of this story by glorifying and praising Him for His mighty, miraculous power, and I have done my very best to do just that.

Next, of course, I want to thank Kevin Zimmerman for being so sensitive to God's Spirit in choosing me to write his story. It was Kevin who first felt urged by God to share his miraculous story with the rest of the world, and it was he, too, who determined that God had chosen me to be the writer of this story.

I had my doubts initially, especially, when one hurdle after another sprang up in front of me, not least of which was my transition from the active Army chaplaincy to the full-time civilian parish and part-time U. S. Army Reserve chaplaincy, and then back into the Alabama Army National Guard chaplaincy, coming full circle to where I had served several years prior. Through it all, Kevin remained steadfast and patient in his conviction that God had chosen me to be the writer and that it would be completed in God's Own good time. Looking back now, however, there is no mistaking God's touch upon Kevin, me, and the whole writing process. The finished product bears true witness and evidence that God was indeed involved with it every step of the way. Praise God!

Naturally, there is more than one vantage point to every story, and Kevin's comrades from the Army helped immeasurably with fleshing out the story from their perspectives. Fellow medic, Joe Sands, and helicopter pilot, David White (no known relation to me), are both due a great debt of gratitude from me for helping to tell this story as it needed to be told. God certainly used each one of them for that purpose. Bishop John Neal's writing of the foreword was very gracious, too.

Finally, I would certainly be remiss if I did not thank my family and friends who have given me their personal and spiritual support while writing this book and taking on this grand adventure of Christian publishing. It has truly been a blessing.

As I finish the updates for this second edition, I am preparing to retire from the United Methodist Church in December 2011 and from the Alabama Army National Guard in February 2012 in order to embark upon an entirely new pastoral ministry venture. I believe God is leading me in this new direction, and the support of my family and friends means more to me now than ever. I pray God's richest blessings upon you all. I don't know exactly what God has in store for us, but I am wholly convinced it will be nothing short of amazing. I can hardly wait to see it come to pass! To God be the glory!

March 2008 (first edition)
October 2011 (revised for 2nd edition)
Rev. Michael L. White
Mobile, Alabama

Foreword

All my life I have admired people of faith and courage who live their lives in the shadows, never seeking notoriety, special favor, or fortune. Many times, they feel the pressure of overwhelming responsibility, yet they handle it without seeking to be noticed. In a world that is over-populated with prideful, self-promoting people, a story of a true public servant and Good Samaritan is easily over-looked. They do great work, thanks to their God-given abilities and seasoned experience. Many fill significant roles and contribute greatly to the accomplishment of critical tasks, all the while remaining virtually anonymous. Without applause, and usually without public awareness, these faithful men and women keep doing what they do, knowing that their names will never be in lights. Quite frankly, they would feel uncomfortable if they were. All the lights and cameras – attention and acknow-ledgements – make them nervous. They don't do what they do to be noticed or to call attention to themselves; they do it because it is their duty. Better stated, it is their calling – it is who they are! Inconspicuously, and most efficiently, they serve and give of themselves. Because of them, the world is a much better place.

As a retired senior Army officer and commander, I've officiated at many retirement ceremonies, and the most requested song dedicated to the retiree's spouse is: "The Wind Beneath My Wings." They are the unsung heroes in the battle, the folks who do the work behind the scenes, the people who pick up the pieces, the ones who make sure everything "under-the-hood" works without a hitch. Frankly, if you take the time to read this book, you will find that Kevin Zimmerman is one of these fascinating individuals with stories to tell that hold you in rapt attention.

When I was asked to write the foreword to this book and given the manuscript, I was speechless! You see, Kevin Zimmerman was more than a soldier that I had a causal relationship with in Germany. In the early to mid-nineties, during the actual time that most of these events occurred, I was also his spiritual leader and pastor. He was more than just one of the church members; he was one of my lead Elders. Frequently, we talked about a myriad of subjects, and not once did he even mention that he was an American Hero.

As a retired combat veteran and commander myself, I have a great appreciation and unique understanding for the degree of courage and selflessness required to respond as Kevin did under these extremely stressful and arduous conditions. I salute this mighty man of valor who continued to put himself in harm's way to help his fellow man. Jesus said, "Greater love hath no man than this, that a man lay down his life for his friends" (John 15:13 KJV). As you read Kevin's story, I pray that you will be inspired, and even compelled, to join the ranks of the many heroes that work silently in the shadows and behind the scenes everyday to make this world a better place to live.

Bishop J. Alan Neal
Agape Christian Faith Center
Ramstein-Miesenbach, Germany

Prologue

When the actual events which inspired this true story began in December 1995, I was preparing to submit my application for active duty Army Chaplaincy for the second time. A series of delays that fit into God's timetable had wrought this circumstance. It had been nearly 12 years since I had left the Army as a SPC (Specialist, E-4), and now, I was attempting to return as a captain and chaplain[1]. I had served all but three weeks of those 12 years in the Alabama Army National Guard, while simultaneously serving as pastor for small, rural congregations throughout southern Alabama. I was notified of my accession into the Army in February 1996, and I left for my first assignment as an Army Chaplain at Ft. Sill, Oklahoma, in early June of that year. At last, God's plan was moving me in a new direction.

Since Kevin Zimmerman and I had never crossed paths prior to beginning the writing of this book, there was absolutely no way for either of us to know what was happening in the other's life. Like the multitudes of other human beings on planet earth, we were simply going about our daily lives doing the best we could. I always marvel at how Almighty God has woven His creation together (including every human being) into one enormous, beautiful tapestry.

Because Kevin is a little more than a year older than I, he chose to enter the Army a year ahead of me at about the same point in his life as I did in mine, i.e., we both entered the Army at about the same age and with some college experience. I am deeply intrigued by the similarities between our military careers and the common places each has taken us, completely independent from the other. Out of the numerous assignments of our separate careers, we share three locations in common: Ft. Jackson, South Carolina; South Korea; and Ft. Sill, Oklahoma. Furthermore, we both went to Korea from Ft. Sill. How coincidental is *that*? I can only conclude that all this commonality, and my 30-plus years of military experience, helps me, as Kevin's writer, to better understand where he was, how he felt, and what he endured. Hopefully, because of that experience, I can relate his story to you more accurately.

Fast-forward now to July 2005. Kevin first contacted me at that time about his search for someone to write a book about the miraculous events he experienced in Bosnia almost ten years earlier. I had published my first book, *Digital Evangelism*, a few months earlier, in October 2004, using the offset press method, and I had just re-released my book by means of the print-on-demand publishing method. The timing was perfect, as my newfound knowledge and insight about this process, along with my many years of Army service and my spiritual convictions, convinced Kevin that I was the right man for the job. It was all a "God thing," of course.

As soon as we agreed I would be the writer, I immediately began contemplating how to lay out the story for the reader. I believe God gave me a revelation as to how to do that. Shortly after I began thinking about it, the idea of times and seasons in life crossed my mind. Instantly, King Solomon's words in the book of Ecclesiastes came to me. There is a time for everything, and, like everyone else, there certainly were several times and seasons that made up Kevin's life. I chose the title from this phrasing and adapted the chapters of this book from several of those times and seasons mentioned in that passage of Scripture. You can read the full pericope at the end of this Prologue.

While Kevin wanted to share how God had demonstrated His miraculous power at strategic times in his life, there are other parts of his life that are too personal to share, and one person from his life has expressed a desire not to be named. Therefore, to honor this request, Kevin's former wife has been renamed to protect her privacy. Moreover, we have maintained this same concern for the privacy of his first fiancée, the mother of his daughter, Niesha.

At the time I agreed to take on the project of writing Kevin's story, my future was rather tumultuous. I was preparing to leave active duty with the Army and return to full-time civilian parish ministry and part-time Army Reserve chaplaincy. I was disheartened at being rejected for promotion by the active Army, but I believed God must have a bigger and better plan for me. I suppose establishing my own Christian publishing house and being able to devote more time and attention to writing Kevin's story was definitely part of that plan.

While the transition from full-time Army Chaplain ministry to full-time civilian parish ministry initially soaked up more of my time and energy than I expected, I eventually settled in, received an amazing degree of inspiration from God, and began writing this story in earnest.

Nearly three years after Kevin and I began this journey toward publication in 2005, it finally came to fruition in 2008. Like the rest of Kevin's life (and mine, too), the writing (and now the update) of this story has been a time and a season for both of us. I pray that in reading it, you will be as blessed as Kevin has been in living it and as I have been in writing it. Before you begin, however, be sure to read the following Scripture passage completely, as it provides the basic structure for the entire story.

Ecclesiastes 3:1-8 KJV

(1) To everything there is a season, and a time to every purpose under the heaven:

(2) A time to be born, and a time to die; a time to plant, and a time to pluck up that which is planted;

(3) A time to kill, and a time to heal; a time to break down, and a time to build up;

(4) A time to weep, and a time to laugh; a time to mourn, and a time to dance;

(5) A time to cast away stones, and a time to gather stones together; a time to embrace, and a time to refrain from embracing;

(6) A time to get, and a time to lose; a time to keep, and a time to cast away;

(7) A time to rend, and a time to sew; a time to keep silence, and a time to speak;

(8) A time to love, and a time to hate; a time of war, and a time of peace.

Chapter One
A Time to Heal

Staff Sergeant Kevin Zimmerman looked intently out the helicopter window as it made a final fly-by in formation with three others. He tried to catch one last glimpse of his beloved family waving goodbye. He thought he saw them, but the chopper sped by so swiftly that he wasn't quite sure. A painful twist seized his stomach, and he choked back tears as the aircraft soared off into the heavens. It was only a few more days until Christmas 1995.

This was yet another Christmas deployment. The U. S. Army has a very bad habit of deploying its service members only days or weeks before this very important of Christian holy days. The stark contrast of instigating war against the backdrop of a season which pronounces "Peace on earth, good will toward men" is hard to miss.

This new deployment brought back memories not yet faded from just a few years prior when Kevin had headed off to the desert to put Saddam Hussein back in his borders. This time, it was a different part of the world – Bosnia.

When he learned of his assignment to Germany, Kevin had no inkling of what lay ahead. With the Cold War over, duty in Western Europe had become much more relaxed. True, there was still a fair amount of field training, but the edge was more or less removed. There was no longer the Soviet Communist threat that had existed for decades prior, and most of the former Eastern Block countries were regaining their independence. All in all, he had been looking forward to serving in Germany, and there was no way for him to know that a tour in Western Europe would eventually mean a tour in Eastern Europe.

After some time in the air, the chopper landed for refueling and a layover. Then it was back in the air. In all, the flight took three days, ferrying its passengers over the Swiss Alps and other spectacular terrain, made all the more so by their beautiful snow covering. Kevin and his fellow soldiers stared out the windows with pensive admiration, while thoughts of "I'm dreaming of a white Christmas" played in their heads.

They arrived at their destination around 5:00 p.m. on Christmas Eve. It was a deeply disturbing sight in the fading light. The war-torn landscape boasted no beautiful architecture, nothing of the familiar cities they had just departed. What buildings were not completely demolished were severely damaged by artillery and pocked by small arms fire.

The roads were eerily deserted. There were no children happily playing around the yards of their homes, no signs of normalcy we all take for granted. The figure of an occasional old woman taking in the wash was all that Kevin saw.

After landing at Camp Eagle, their area head-quarters in Bosnia, they were ordered to collect their gear and disembark. There was no welcoming party – just a singular officer, who directed them to their temporary quarters. He gave them one final announcement before they parted.

"Oh, yeah, and don't forget that we will have a special lunchtime meal for Christmas tomorrow. The DFAC opens at 1130 sharp and closes at 1300, so don't miss it."

That was it. They had officially arrived, and now all that remained was to count down the days till time to go home, and, of course, to do the jobs they were sent here to do.

In Kevin's case, that meant service as a flight medic, assisting the doctors and nurses in caring for the wounded and injured. He had no idea right now just what all that would entail.

Aside from the special lunchtime meal, Christmas Day proved to be a day like any other in the Army, especially at a forward deployed site like

Camp Eagle. The camaraderie with fellow troops was what made the day truly special, however. They all found themselves sharing in the common bond of military service at the edge of the field of battle. Christmas Day, or any day, made little difference to that fact.

The ensuing days and weeks gradually drifted into routine. Just three days after arriving at Camp Eagle, Kevin and the rest of his company, the 236th Ambulance Company, who arrived later, were transferred to a neighboring site they dubbed "The Blue Factory," because of its blue buildings.

Being the devoted Christian that he was, Kevin soon sought out the nearest chapel for religious services shortly after his arrival. He knew he could not go long without spiritual replenishment. However, he quickly learned there was no chaplain co-located at their installation to conduct services for them. Although the chaplain was able to visit them on a few occasions, he lived at a neighboring camp, called Tuzla Main, a few miles away, so conducting religious services would be a challenge.

Kevin obtained permission to organize services for himself and his fellow soldiers, as well as a weekly Bible study. While he conducted some of the services and Bible studies himself, there were other soldiers with both the ability and the willingness who usually led them.

The Army has a variety of faith groups represented, and within those groups, a variety of worship styles, too. Among Christians, there are the Roman Catholic, Eastern Orthodox, and Protestant groups. Within the Protestant groups, there is the plain vanilla, Collective Protestant Service, which caters to all Protestant denominations who wish to attend, and there are a few denominationally-specific Christians who, because of strong traditions, rituals, and denominational requirements, hold their own individual services.

For instance, the Episcopal, Lutheran, Pentecostal, Gospel, and Church of Christ services are generally held separately from the Collective Protestant services, assuming a chaplain or denominational leader, what the Army chaplain corps calls a "distinctive faith group leader" (or DFGL, for short), is available to conduct such a service. Since the chaplain providing religious support for the 236th Air Ambulance was conducting services at Tuzla Main on Sundays, he was unable to conduct a service for them on Sundays, because traveling to that site was rather difficult. Therefore, Kevin organized a Gospel service for his comrades and arranged for preachers from among their own membership. Although it was a small congregation, averaging fifteen each Sunday, it was a vital part of life for the soldiers stationed at The Blue Factory.

After settling in to their home away from home and organizing the weekly worship and Bible studies, the soldiers' lives began to take on a routine of daily living. During the week, they worked in shifts, remaining on-call for whatever medical emergencies, or non-emergencies in some cases, that arose. They shared this duty with some Norwegian service members serving with the U. N. peace-keeping force.

After the first few weeks had passed since their arrival, the memory of the Christmas and New Year's holidays quickly faded into the past. Time was really starting to tick down now.

The morning of January 14, 1996, started like any other. The weather was cold and rainy, but there was nothing in the air to give any sense of foreboding to anyone. Kevin was on call as "second-up," which meant his team was the second tier, or backup, for the primary, or "first-up," team. Everyone was going about his routine like every other day.

Suddenly, the PA speaker blared,

"MEDEVAC! MEDEVAC! MEDEVAC!"

Everyone's heart skipped a beat, and then they sprang into action. Kevin's good buddy, Sergeant Joe Sands, was on the first-up team, and he raced downstairs to the orderly room to meet with his PIC and locate their destination on the map. Kevin ran down there, too, to see if his help might be needed.

The report came in that a Swiss APC had struck an anti-tank landmine. There were nine injured: two critical, one serious, and six walking wounded. This would require both medical teams at the scene.

The two UH-60 Blackhawks' pre-flight checks and all other equipment checks were done first thing that morning, so all that was necessary now was to hop onboard, start up the engine, and take off. It took several minutes to arrive, but due to the adrenalin rush, it seemed to Joe like mere seconds.

Flying above the scene, they saw what appeared to be Muslim troops entrenched at the top of the hill, while gray-clad, uniformed Serbian troops were entrenched at the bottom of the hill. In between the two wound an unpaved road, and as they circled over it in their chopper, the outline of an immense crater came into view. The pilot could not land on the roadway now for fear of more land-mines, and hoist operations were not an option, because of the weather and proximity to the mountainside, so he finally found a landing site about 500 yards away. As the realization crossed his mind, Joe spoke to the crew chief, Sergeant Forester, through the aircraft's helmet communication system,

"Tell me I'm not gonna have to walk that road!"

As Joe's helicopter lifted off to allow Kevin's helicopter to land and let him off, Joe had already headed up the road. The rain continued to fall steadily, but just a little lighter than a downpour. Tiny rivulets streamed through tire tracks from the day before, and Joe's footprints were already starting to wash out of sight. Kevin swallowed hard and started the trek up the hill, following the tire tracks and footprints as well as he could, uncertain if they were actually tracks anymore.

The commanding officer of the Swiss soldiers met Kevin just after he disembarked and spoke urgently to him. He said,

"You have to get up there and save my men! If you don't, they will die!"

As it turned out, he was the only one in the group that could speak English. This distressed plea spurred Kevin onward.

As he picked his way up the road, some of the landmines were now visible, exposed by the rain, but that only worried him about the ones that were still hidden. Once he started up the road, however, the thought never crossed his mind to turn back.

When he arrived at the scene, he traversed the crater and approached Joe. He asked,

"Joe, man, whatchya got? How can I help?"

Joe directed him to help with one of the critical patients and the two walking wounded. They set to work frantically binding wounds and preparing the soldiers for transport. Limbs that once felt firm now felt like packaged hamburger. Unfortunately, those limbs would be lost.

A Norwegian heavy ambulance, dispatched at the same time as the choppers, arrived, and they began helping to load the most seriously injured soldiers onto stretchers. Then they helped transport them back down the road to the waiting helicopters.

With all the pressure of the day's events, Joe walked somewhat dazedly back down the road, aimlessly crisscrossing it, and mindlessly unaware of the danger he was flirting with. Kevin yelled at him,

"Joe, what are you doing? Stop walking outside the footprints!"

This jolted him back to reality and sobered him up in an instant. He shuddered at the realization of what he had just done. As he would later say on reflection,

"That was not the last time, or even the most important time, Kevin stopped me from wandering aimlessly."

They arrived back at the waiting choppers in practically no time and climbed aboard with their wounded human cargo. There was no time even to think about what they had just gone through. It was not until after they had returned to base and began to unwind that the full extent of their experience came to light.

An ordnance officer was dispatched to assess the situation of the mined roadway. He stopped by The Blue Factory to give his report. They met in the DFAC. The 236th Air Ambulance's company commander asked how many mines were in that area, and the ordnance officer replied,

"It was a miracle. Your men were not supposed to get in and out of there."

He next reached for a salt shaker, poured some salt onto his palm, and then threw the salt onto the table. He said,

"That many. If you can count it, you're better than we are."

The full magnitude of their miraculous experience now hit home. Kevin knew it was the hand of God, and Joe, an uncommitted, nominal believer prior to that, now knew it, too.

As he continued to reflect upon the goodness of God in his life, Kevin could not help now but to look back upon how his faith in God had started. Memories came flooding into his mind, and people and events that he had not thought about in years began to parade in front of his mind's eye. Voices from his parents, grandparents, teachers, leaders, and other significant people echoed in his mind. It was quite a sight to behold.

Chapter Two
A Time to Be Born

On February 4, 1960, at a hospital in Toledo, Ohio, Verna Zimmerman cradled her seventh and last child, Kevin, just a short while after giving birth to him. Her husband, Oscar, looked on with great pride and joy, as nearly every husband and father does. Even after seven times, the miracle of life still left them awestruck at how a tiny human being could arrive in this world from a simple act of love. The nine-plus months of waiting and anticipating, of preparing and praying for good health, were no less present with this seventh child than with their first. They grinned and gazed at him with high hopes for his future.

Oscar and Verna were truly devoted parents, determined to provide for all their children's needs with all their meager means. Oscar worked hard at manual labor as a construction worker for much of his life. He was a quiet man who, like so many others of his generation, was not always obvious with his affections, but he was a deeply caring man nonetheless.

Verna often worked at multiple jobs doing whatever she could find, mostly as a waitress or a housekeeper. She did this because she wanted her children to enjoy some of the things in life she was unable to have for herself.

It was a hard life for Oscar and Verna, but it was a living. Their family never wanted for any of the necessities of life. There was always enough to eat, decent clothes to wear, and a comfortable home to live in.

While Oscar was a very quiet, reserved man, Verna was just the opposite. She was very affect-tionate and quite vocal at times. She also handled most of the discipline in the household. Through-out his childhood, Kevin remembered numerous occasions where one moment his mother would be singing the praises of her children to another parent, only to turn and sharply correct them for their misbehavior in the next moment. It was hard to miss the humor in the sharp contrast.

By the time Kevin was old enough to remember, his oldest siblings were preparing to leave home. Consequently, he had limited contact with them while growing up, but he believed his family to be rather close-knit, just the same.

He was especially close to his grandparents, who lived just two doors down from him during his childhood. Visiting with them was a part of his daily routine. Their role in his upbringing was also quite influential.

Perhaps their greatest influence was in his spiritual life. While his parents were believers, they got so caught up in the business of making a living that they sometimes failed to attend to the most important aspect of their children's lives, their relationship with Jesus Christ. Leave it to God, however, to insure that those He calls are afforded every opportunity to choose eternal life with Him.

Grandma and Grandpa Suttler, affectionately known as Big Mama and Big Daddy to all their grandchildren, saw to it that their grandchildren, and Kevin among them, were in church on Sundays. It was an experience which would shape Kevin's life in ways he would not realize for years to come.

Despite their meager earnings, Oscar and Verna managed to send their children to some of the best parochial schools available to them. Kevin and his next older sister, Kendra, nick-named Candy, spent kindergarten through third grade at St. Philip's Lutheran Academy. They attended fourth through eighth grades at St. Theresa's Catholic School, in the heart of Toledo's inner city. Each of these schools had a very diverse student body, which left Kevin with rather unrealistic expectations for his high school years.

When it came time for him to begin high school, Verna had big plans for Kevin. She planned to enroll him in Toledo Central Catholic High School, a predominantly White school. From the moment he walked through the doors on orientation day, the culture shock was almost more than Kevin could bear. He scanned the crowd of faces gathered there for just one Black face, but the search was in vain. For the first time in his life, he felt out of place. He began to protest to his mother that this was an unacceptable option for him, but she simply ignored his pleas.

While prejudice was not taught in his family, Kevin could not ignore its strong presence in the turmoil of the sixties and seventies while he was growing up. There were very few White people in his neighborhood, and he had previously attended school with one or two of them, but none of them behaved toward him as any of the Whites he had observed in the news on television or heard about in personal conversations with others. It was indeed a confusing time for him.

After Verna enrolled Kevin in Toledo Central Catholic, against his will, of course, she took him aside to a secluded spot to talk about it. The conversation that ensued is burned into his heart even to this day.

"Son, I want you to *always* be proud of who and what you are. *Never* be ashamed of being Black! God made you just the way you are, just like He made everybody else just the way they are. Do you remember everything you've ever learned about God in your life, about Him being no respecter of persons, and loving everybody alike? Do you honestly believe all that's true?"

Kevin nodded in silence.

"Well, then, remember this: no matter what some people do to other people, God made all kinds of people, and He didn't make any mistakes. The White people you see in this school are no different from you. You've got to understand that

that means you are no less and no better than anybody else in this school. Remember that God made us all, and God loves us all. Therefore, He expects us to learn how to love each other, just as He loves us. So, for you, my son, learning to deal with all kinds of people starts right now. Now, go, and make your Mama proud!"

This little heart-to-heart talk ultimately shaped how Kevin would view other races for the rest of his life, and, coupled with his eventual, positive experience at Toledo Central Catholic, his high school years showed him an entirely different view of the White race than what was portrayed in his community and on the evening news.

Much to Kevin's relief, however, God provided a few other Black students to keep him from feeling completely foreign. Kevin, Glen, Earl, and Melissa all became inseparable friends.

Racial acceptance was finally proven to Kevin when he earned the starting running back position on the freshman football team. Glen earned the starting defensive back position. Cordell, another Black student, also earned a place on the team. The remaining members of the team were White players.

This team would eventually serve as the grand platform for racial equality in Kevin's young life, as the entire team was united in the goal of winning. They came together and worked hard in both practice and in all the games. Their efforts rewarded them with victory after victory, and finally, the co-championship of the city that year. This, in turn, won Kevin his place as the starting running back for the varsity squad the remaining three years he attended Toledo Central Catholic. His success brought him popularity, and his popularity brought him more interaction with both races.

In retrospect, it is clear how God was developing Kevin's character to overcome the petty misunderstandings that often arise out of ignorance about the different races. Perhaps God did the same with the other students who attended there, as well. While there were some occasional indications of prejudice from both White and Black students, Toledo Central Catholic's zero tolerance policy quickly restored the vision of interpersonal harmony that only a truly yielded life in Christ can consistently provide.

Kevin's remaining high school years flew by, and before he knew it, it was time for college. After spending so much money on private Christian education, Kevin wanted to prove to his parents that he could obtain just as good an education by spending less money at a state school, so he chose Tennessee State University to save them money. He decided to major in medical technology. In order to focus more intently on his studies, however, Kevin chose not to play football in college. Instead, he got involved in the school's student politics. He ran for and won election to the office of freshman class president. It was truly a joy to accomplish such a feat in his first year in college, and in a college located in another state at that. The glorious future Kevin's parents had planned for him seemed to be unfolding before his very eyes. Life was truly good, but that was about to change.

During Christmas break, Kevin returned home to celebrate the holidays with his family and to be reunited with his girlfriend, who had been attending a different college. The past few months of separation had proved difficult for them both, though they believed they had coped well enough with it. Nevertheless, in their joy of being together again, and in a moment of uncontrolled, unprotected passion, they conceived their first and only child, Niesha. In an instant, the direction of their lives was changed.

Since he didn't learn this news until he had returned to school, Kevin decided to finish the remainder of his freshman year at Tennessee State, but he was determined to take full responsibility for his child. Although his girlfriend was still living with her parents, and Kevin was still living with his parents, he did not want either his parents or his girlfriend's parents to pay for what he believed to be his personal obligation.

He dropped out of college at the end of that semester and went to work at a local housing manufacturing plant in Toledo. However, in just three months' time, they announced they were going out of business. It was a pretty big setback.

The next four months proved to be among the hardest of Kevin's whole life. With limited job skills and an incomplete education, he struggled to find work with an adequate income to provide enough money just to buy the disposable diapers for Niesha, let alone provide for her other needs. Yet, the worst was still to come.

During this time, he had finally landed a job working at a fast-food restaurant flipping burgers. It was obvious the manager had no experience with how to properly supervise his employees. The worst of it, though, was how the manager constantly belittled his workers.

After about three months of daily, verbal abuse, Kevin had endured all he could. In the midst of a large, lunchtime crowd, the manager made Kevin the focus of his ire, cursing at him and accusing him of being too slow at his job. Kevin had swallowed his pride time and again on previous occasions, but it finally came back up with a vengeance. He glared sternly at the manager and yelled,

"If you curse me one more time, you'll be cookin' these burgers your *@#! self!"

As soon as he had said it, Kevin was sorry he had used an expletive, but he felt he needed to say what he had said. Unphased, the arrogant manager challenged Kevin's young manhood, and retorted,

"You'll keep cookin' till I tell you to quit!"

By this time, the whole restaurant was eyeing this most unseemly and unprofessional display.

Kevin tore off his apron, threw his hat to the floor, and said,

"Watch me!"

The whole crowd cheered and slapped him on the back as he marched triumphantly out the door. It felt good for the moment to get that pent-up anger and resentment off his chest, but walking home, he pondered what he would do now. Rather than feeling proud for standing up for himself, he felt he had hit rock bottom in his life.

As he walked home, Kevin thought about his options. How would he provide for his little daughter? For a while, he considered whether he should do what so many other hopeless, young men of the inner city had done – turn to a life on the streets. A life of crime appeared to be quite appealing in his time of desperation.

As he sat dejected in front of his television, a commercial came on the screen. The message: "Be all you can be." While this was an advertisement for the Army, Kevin thought of how proud he was of his older brother, James, who was serving in the Air Force. He thought to himself,

"I'll join the Air Force, like my brother."

The next morning, he rose early and headed for the recruiting station. The Air Force recruiter arranged for him to take the qualifying test, and within three days, he took the ASVAB test.

At long last, he felt he had found the solution to his problems. What happened next, however, would test his resolve and send him in a direction he could not have imagined.

Chapter Three
A Time to Build Up

The few days it took to get back the results of the ASVAB seemed like an eternity to Kevin. When the Air Force recruiter called to give him the news, he was unprepared for the answer.

"I'm sorry to have to tell you this, but you failed the test."

Kevin's heart sank. How could he have failed? he wondered. His ego was bruised. The recruiter continued,

"Now, that's not unusual. Lots of people fail the ASVAB. We'll just get you some study materials and reschedule you to take it again."

Kevin agreed to retake the test, since he felt this was his best opportunity to provide for his foundling family and avoid a life on the streets. Some days later, the recruiter called again with the same result. Kevin could hardly believe his ears.

He decided to see if he would get a different result from the Army recruiter, so he went through the same procedure with him. Just as he was about to take the next step in the Army recruiter's office, the Air Force recruiter poked his head in the door and asked to speak with the Army recruiter. Though they had stepped out into the hallway, Kevin still overheard his name being used more than once, so he decided to inquire as to what was happening.

As it turned out, the Air Force recruiter had mixed up the test results. The failures were actually someone else's. Kevin had, in fact, passed the test both times. The recruiter smiled broadly, thinking this news would bring great joy to Kevin. Apparently, the Air Force recruiter's main concern was his recruiting numbers, but all Kevin could think about was the humiliation he had endured not once, but twice. Kevin turned to the Army recruiter and said,

"At least, you felt my future was important enough not to mix me up. I'm goin' Army."

A few weeks later, in November 1980, Kevin found himself at Ft. Jackson, South Carolina, for basic combat training. The culture shock was as pronounced as it could be.

When Kevin's bus first arrived, a drill sergeant stepped aboard and began screaming orders to the occupants to grab their gear and get off the bus immediately. As Kevin exited the bus, the drill sergeant stepped directly into his path, causing Kevin to bump into him. Instantly, the drill sergeant began yelling about him hitting a superior officer and having to go to jail for it. When Kevin tried to apologize, the drill sergeant then screamed that he was speaking without permission. The drill sergeant asked,

"Where you from, Private?"

Kevin yelled, "Toledo, Ohio, sir!"

"Do I look like an officer to you, Private? Don't call me 'sir'; I work for a living!"

Kevin thought whatever answers he gave would be wrong, so he decided not to say anything. This was a mistake, too. The drill sergeant barked at him again.

"So, we have ourselves a city slicker, huh?"

Kevin tried to reply, "I'm from the city …", but the drill sergeant cut him off.

"Drop and give me 50!"

Kevin dropped down into the push-up position and began doing push-ups. He had done only two or three when the drill sergeant yelled at him again.

"Get on your feet, Private!"

By this time, everyone else was arranged into two separate formations, one all male, the other all female. Kevin didn't know when or from where the females had arrived. There were other drill sergeants now standing in front of these two formations, in addition to Drill Sergeant Bee, who had been drilling Kevin from the start.

Drill Sergeant Bee walked in circles around Kevin, as he addressed the whole group.

"When I address you, you will respond as loud as you can with "Yes, Drill Sergeant! No, Drill Sergeant! Do you hear me?"

Kevin shouted, "Yes, Drill Sergeant!"

Drill Sergeant Bee yelled at the others in formation, "Do you think I'm talking only to this Private?"

Everyone then shouted, "No, Drill Sergeant!"

Drill Sergeant Bee continued, "When you do push-ups here, you will count, 'One, Drill Sergeant, two, Drill Sergeant!' Now drop and give me 50!"

Kevin immediately followed his instructions, while the others remained standing. Drill Sergeant Bee then screamed,

"DO YOU THINK I'M TALKING ONLY TO HIM?!"

Everyone shouted, "No, Drill Sergeant" and began doing push-ups. Drill Sergeant Bee then said,

"Don't do 50; keep pushin' until I get tired!"

Kevin then lost the hope of finishing before everyone else and getting a breather. Drill Sergeant Bee turned this into a class on the proper posture and method of doing the push-up, and the other drill sergeants went from recruit to recruit coaching them on their technique.

The rest of the day became a blur. Kevin remembered doing some in-processing paper-work, but little else. By the end of the day, they were all thoroughly exhausted.

The next day, around 4:00 a.m., the lights flashed on in the barracks, and a lot of screaming and loud banging on large, metal trash cans roused everyone from their sound sleep. This is one of the drill sergeants' favorite times of the day, especially with a new group of raw recruits.

Everyone began rushing to get dressed and hurry outside to formation. As Kevin was about to head out the door, he suddenly noticed his bunk mate in the bunk above him, who had yet to move a muscle. Kevin ran back to try and wake him. He said,

"Hey, man, you gotta get up and get to formation!", but the young man simply looked at Kevin, smiled, and said,

"Nope."

Kevin was stunned. "What d'you mean, 'Nope'?"

"Kev," he said, "I'm going back to Alabama."

Just then, Drill Sergeant Bee entered the room checking for stragglers. Everyone else was already outside.

"What's going on here?"

"Nothing, Drill Sergeant," Kevin replied.

Drill Sergeant Bee now addressed the other Private. "What are you doing here, Private? Why aren't you out in formation?"

"Just wanna go home, Drill Sergeant."

"Private Zimmerman, what are you doing here?"

The other Private answered for Kevin. "Because of me, Drill Sergeant. He came back to get me to fall out with everybody else."

Drill Sergeant Bee told Kevin to get out of there and go to formation, which he did immediately. However, as soon as he got into the formation, another drill sergeant, though a little softer-spoken, called out in a very stern voice,

"Who is that that just fell into my formation late?"

Kevin knew he was talking about him, so he replied,

"Private Zimmerman, Drill Sergeant!"

"Private Zimmerman, front and center."

Kevin then saw Senior Drill Sergeant Cruz for the first time. He was a short, Hispanic man. He was in charge of the other drill sergeants, and his demeanor showed that he obviously didn't play games.

Drill Sergeant Cruz approached Kevin's platoon and gave the command, "Half-right, face!"

Of course, since they had not yet been trained in drill and ceremony, some turned halfway to the right, others faced completely to the right, and the rest simply turned their heads to the right. Drill Sergeant Cruz then took this opportunity for another impromptu instruction, like the ones the previous day regarding appropriate response to a drill sergeant and how to properly do push-ups. It was just another of many they would endure over the coming weeks.

This current class was shorter, however, as Drill Sergeant Cruz wanted to place more emphasis on the lesson of teamwork, so he soon ordered everyone in the platoon to the front leaning rest position for push-ups. He made the point that if one member of the team was late, the whole team was late.

While they were doing their push-ups, Drill Sergeant Bee arrived and pulled Drill Sergeant Cruz to the side, where he explained to him why Kevin was late. Drill Sergeant Cruz then gave the commands,

"Halt! Position of attention, move! Half-left, face!" Everyone stopped their push-ups, got to their feet, and, due to the recent lesson on proper facing movements, got the half-left command right this time.

Drill Sergeant Cruz then explained to the group how Kevin's bunk mate had quit, and how Kevin had risked punishment to go back and urge his bunk mate to make it to formation, but he said nothing else about the subject.

While the drill sergeants never said what happened to Kevin's bunk mate, he was likely given a general discharge and sent home, though it is also possible he could have gone to jail en route to his home. Refusing to train is a dishonorable behavior, and any discharge other than an Honorable one is a disgrace and frequently results in loss of employment opportunities later in life, especially if those jobs are in the government.

Due to Kevin's honorable behavior, Drill Sergeant Cruz said to him in front of the whole formation, while Kevin continued to stand out front,

"Because of your actions, you're already standing in the right place. You will be the first Platoon Guide for your platoon."

It turned out to be a heavy responsibility which required being the first-up and the last to bed everyday. While he felt honored to hold the position, Kevin soon discovered the meaning of Jesus' words, "To whom much is given, much is required." He learned to manage all kinds of responsibility and to adjust to plans that didn't go accordingly. He also learned that not everyone would respect him or his position, though he commanded respect, because he gave it. He held this post for the first full week of training, before it was passed along to another in the weekly rotation.

After this shocking beginning, an experience which is repeated by fresh recruits to the Army at the start of every new training cycle, the remainder of basic training settled down into a routine that is pretty much the same for every other recruit who goes through the system. Classes on drill and ceremony, first aid, personal hygiene, rifle marksmanship, and so much more rounded out the remaining weeks of training, making for full, busy days nearly every day, including weekends, though an occasional pass might be permitted for good behavior. This rare opportunity would usually mean a trip to the nearest Post Exchange (or PX) for a little browsing around for more stationery and postcards for writing home and a heart-warming phone call to home, providing the waiting line was not too long. It was the same for practically everyone.

The eight weeks of basic combat training ticked by in what seemed like record time for Kevin. Before he knew it, graduation day arrived, and he was preparing to catch a flight to Ft. Sam Houston, in San Antonio, Texas, for his Advanced Initial Training (AIT) as a combat medic.

Much like the experience Kevin had going from St. Theresa Catholic School to Toledo Central Catholic High School, Ft. Sam Houston's quasi-civilian, school campus lifestyle was not an accurate picture of life elsewhere in the Army. Kevin thought it was just like college, except he had to wear an Army uniform. When classes were over in the afternoon, students were allowed to change into civilian clothes, interact with both males and females, and go and come as they desired, provided they did not go beyond a certain distance and were back in time for the next day's classes. Given that unrealistically relaxed perspective, Kevin thought to himself, "If this is what the Army is like, I *know* I'm gonna do 20 years!"

He enjoyed learning about medical subjects, and he had fun touring some of the local sights around San Antonio, too. Although he had plenty of opportunities for shopping, he spent very little money, because he sent most of it home to help with his little daughter's needs.

In the few weeks it took him to complete his combat medic AIT, Kevin was eager to move on. He finally had a skill and a job with an income, albeit a meager one, with which to perform that skill. He was now ready to provide full time for his foundling family.

Upon completing AIT, Kevin was next assigned to a field artillery unit at Ft. Sill, Oklahoma. Sometime later, it became apparent to him that his girlfriend's affections for him had diminished so significantly that they would not spend their lives together after all. Even more regrettable, he would miss out on their daughter's rearing and lose his influence in her upbringing. It was an excruciatingly painful experience for Kevin in many ways.

In recalling the Scripture that says "…all things work together for good to them that love God, to them who are the called according to his purpose" (Romans 8:28 KJV), Kevin realized that, despite the pain and heartache he was suffering for this failed relationship, his daughter, Niesha, was the good that God had worked out of it all. From that understanding, he took great comfort. Eventually, he hoped to experience love again.

Chapter Four
A Time to Love

As Kevin's heart began to heal from the brokenness and disappointment of losing relationship with his former fiancée and baby daughter, he struggled to move on with his life. He had duties and obligations to fulfill, and an Army career to maintain. In time, perhaps he would meet another woman, a sincere Christian, who would make his world complete.

In the meantime, Kevin's Army career continued to progress. He served a total of five years and five months as a medic at Ft. Sill. The first three of those five years he spent in a field artillery unit.

Duty in battalions like these is a singular one, since only one medic is assigned per company, troop, or battery. Since each battalion is usually comprised of three or more companies, troops, or batteries, according to their mission, there would be limited interaction between members of these separate sub-units. Moreover, depending on the level of involvement in unit activities, such as extracurricular sporting events, both individual soldiers in the unit and leaders in the chain of command will base their opinion of such "outsiders" as medics, personnel clerks, and even chaplain assistants on their willingness to participate in such activities. For the strongly introverted or non-athletic, it can mean lack of respect, exclusion, and condescension, often resulting in a very lonely service.

Fortunately for Kevin, his outgoing personality and eagerness to participate quickly earned him the respect and appreciation of practically everyone in his unit. Building rapport like this is the key to having a successful tour of duty in any unit.

To add to this respect, Kevin also participated in Soldier of the Month boards, winning the company level competition three times, the battalion level once, and placing second in the brigade level competition once. This was largely responsible for his fast tracked promotion to the rank of sergeant, too. This served only to further motivate Kevin to pursue greater and greater challenges.

During a field training exercise, not long after his promotion to sergeant, Kevin was relaxing in his tent during a downpour of rain, when a fellow soldier rushed inside, all excited, and shouted,

"Doc, you gotta come quick! Battiste flipped his vehicle and is pinned under it!"

"Doc" is the nickname soldiers give to all their medics, though none of them confuse medics with actual medical doctors. Kevin quickly grabbed his medical kit and raced beside the soldier to a waiting vehicle where they drove to the scene of the accident.

Another medic from one of the other batteries also arrived at the scene around the same time.

They quickly assessed that Battiste's arm was pinned underneath the vehicle, which was lying on its side, and if they did not extricate him soon, he could lose his arm. They agreed to try to lift the vehicle just enough for Battiste to pull himself loose. This plan worked, and as soon as he was free, they immediately evaluated the condition of his injury.

In the meantime, a MEDEVAC chopper had also been dispatched, and it arrived shortly after they finished bandaging Battiste's arm and placing it in a sling. The MEDEVAC medic ushered Battiste to the chopper, whereupon he insured they were both properly restrained, before they flew off to the hospital. Kevin said a quick prayer for his friend, Battiste, as he watched the helicopter fly away.

Watching the flight medic do his job and fly off in what seemed like a blaze of glory sparked Kevin's imagination. He was now quite taken with the duty of a flight medic, so he applied for this new position in Army medicine as soon as he was back in cantonment. He was accepted, and thus began the remaining years of his Army career.

In May 1986, Kevin was reassigned to Taegu, in the Republic of Korea, better known as South Korea to most of us. This is normally a one year tour of duty, but Kevin, who was still single, volunteered to extend for a second year. He had discovered that, aside from the long distance from America and the separation from family, service in Korea is not nearly as bad as its negative reputation. In fact, it is a pretty good experience.

When it was time for his next assignment, he was reassigned to the very same aviation unit he had left just two years prior at Ft. Sill, Oklahoma. He spent the next year and some months performing his duty at the same level of excellence he had now established as his personal standard.

Around this same time, in the summer of 1989, Kevin met Cassandra. It happened purely by

accident one day, as these sorts of "chance" meet-
ings always do. Of course, nothing is ever by
chance or accident when God is involved (see
Proverbs 16:33).

Kevin accompanied one of his fellow soldiers,
a good friend, to a day care located off-post to pick
up his friend's son. Had it not been for accompany-
ing this friend, Kevin would never have set foot
there. While there, however, Kevin could not help
but notice the attractive woman who worked as the
manager. As it turned out, she was also good
friends with his friend's family.

Time passed, and Kevin and Cassandra continued to cross each other's paths, until one day, in a
grocery store parking lot, he asked her out on a
date. She accepted, and six months later, in January
1990, they were married by the Justice of the Peace
in nearby Wichita Falls, Texas, a town located a
few miles south of Ft. Sill. Soon after their first
anniversary, however, they held a small, private,
religious ceremony for their family and friends.

Since Cassandra already had three children of her own, Kevin had an instant family. They spent the next several years laboring together to raise and train them up in the way they should go (Proverbs 22:6).

Their Christian faith became the centerpiece of their personal lives and their family's life. They were constantly on the go, attending many church training conferences and other programs and activities, all of which strengthened their faith. Kevin, in particular, felt his faith grew tremendously during this time, and he feels he owes a great debt of gratitude to Cassandra for her unfailing support and encouragement.

There was never any doubt of their love for one another, despite the many challenges of raising a blended family, and Kevin continued to send financial support to his daughter, Niesha, too. Money was tight, but they still found multiple ways to stretch it to meet their family's needs. Except for the stress of financial worries, their lives were otherwise quite satisfying.

One practice Kevin began with his new family was family Bible study. He was determined to follow the Biblical example of Joshua who said, "...as for me and my house, we will serve the Lord" (Joshua 24:15 KJV). They spent many times in lively discussion of how to apply the Bible to daily living in the modern era. It was indeed a challenging feat.

While having Christian parents who are truly devoted to teaching their children about living the committed Christian life is a definite plus, it is by no means a guarantee of smooth sailing, particularly during the typical teen years. Kevin's new children were certainly no exception. While the youngest was still pre-teen and less influenced by peers, the two older ones were well involved in the youth culture and often questioned the applicability of the Bible's mandates to life today. It proved quite difficult to enforce the Biblical standard in their home, though

Kevin and Cassandra worked very diligently to do so. Attending weekly worship included some resistance, too, from time to time, but it usually did not result in a big hassle. All in all, Kevin and Cassandra managed to maintain a united front against this common assault on their family.

In truth, however, Kevin was more concerned with his actual example of Christian living before his children than with his teaching them what to believe. He reflected often upon what his own father had taught him about personal belief and actual actions. On more than one occasion, Kevin recalled his father saying,

"Son, you will hear people talk a lot. They'll always say what they believe and what they'll do. What I want you to remember is no matter what they say, watch what they do, because people DO what they BELIEVE."

This sage advice remained with Kevin all his life, and it was never more apropos than in parenting. Its impact was especially felt in his household shortly after they attended worship with another church in the area where they lived. One of the teens in that church had been attracted to one of Kevin's teens and wanted to maintain contact. However, the other teen's parents were opposed and asked their pastor to intervene on their behalf. Kevin was understanding about the matter until the pastor explained his reasoning.

"Brother Zimmerman, I need to inform you that you are to keep your child away from my member's child. We do not condone interracial dating in our church."

Kevin was stunned by the statement and said that, while the other parents could require their child to sever communications, he would not require his child to do so. However, after further discussion of the matter with Cassandra, they concluded that they would need to instruct their child on the importance of respecting this other teen's obligation to respect her parents' rules.

It was a truly disheartening experience and was obvious proof that this other pastor and congregation *said* they believed in loving and accepting all people, including all races, but their actions clearly demonstrated that they did not actually *believe* it. It illuminated a painful gap between Christian teaching and actual Christian living that permeates our society even now. Moreover, it also presented a hypocrisy that made it even more difficult for Kevin and Cassandra to teach their children about the genuine love of God for all people. In fact, Kevin asked himself, "How do you teach your children the lyrics of that much-beloved children's hymn, 'Jesus Loves the Little Children of the World,' when a CHURCH discriminates against you?" There appeared to be no easy answer.

Despite the sting of this experience, which lingers even until now, Kevin continued to teach his children that God loves everyone exactly as the Bible says, and he urged them not to stereotype an entire group of people based on the failure of one pastor and one congregation. Though it was not easy, he believes he made some difference with them, just the same.

As time passed, Kevin became more and more involved in his spiritual growth and development by listening to such renowned preachers and teachers as T. D. Jakes, Tony Evans, Mark Hanby, Noel Jones, Eddy Long, and Joyce Meyers, to name a few. Cassandra played an important role by encouraging this growth, too.

Perhaps the one who made the biggest impact on his spiritual life and understanding, however, was Bishop T. D. Jakes. Bishop Jakes explained the human condition in such a way that helped Kevin see how great his need for God's forgiveness and salvation really was. Kevin began to love the idea that God loved him so much, in spite of his imperfection, that He sent Christ to save his soul. It made him hungry to know more.

Kevin became more concerned about making himself accountable for his actions, and while he doesn't claim to have arrived, by any means, he feels his personal character is better today because of the in-depth Christian teaching he underwent then. In fact, due to his growth in knowledge and understanding of God's Word through the years, Kevin now believes that Love is not only something that can be spoken, but Love can be *seen.*

In a highly stressful occupation, such as being an Army medic, this philosophy has proven its powerful value time and again. In fact, Kevin's spiritual growth and understanding during his first ten-and-one-half months of marriage to Cassandra proved to be a very apt preparation from God for what lay just ahead for him, for only God could have fully foreseen Kevin's future.

Chapter Five
A Time for War

Kevin was at the half-way point in his Army career when he and Cassandra were married in 1990. They had been married less than a year, however, when danger loomed on the horizon.

A despot named Saddam Hussein in a country hardly anyone had heard of previously was causing unrest throughout his region. In a single, unilateral act of aggression, he had invaded Kuwait and re-claimed what he purported was territory rightfully belonging to Iraq taken during a previous war.

Military alliances being what they are, the United States was drawn into the conflict at Saudi Arabia's request. President George H. W. Bush built a contingent coalition of international forces and staged them on the border of Saudi Arabia just before Christmas in 1990. His military commanders dubbed the mission Operation Desert Shield.

Being a stubborn and arrogant egotist, Hussein was not about to retreat and relinquish his prize, regardless of either diplomatic or military pressure. After ample warning and some of the widest media coverage of any war in history, complete with CNN reporters meeting U. S. Marines as they beached and prepared to attack, the mission transitioned into Operation Desert Storm on January 17, 1991,[2] and became a full-fledged, armed conflict, now known as The Persian Gulf War.

Kevin's unit, the Fourth Battalion, 507th Air Ambulance, was deployed as part of the First Infantry Division, which arrived in Saudi Arabia on Christmas Day in 1990. It was quite a sight.

As the air war began on January 17, 1991, the ground troops anxiously awaited their turn. Following numerous bombing sorties across Iraq, the commanders believed Saddam Hussein's capabilities were significantly reduced and softened as to better enable their ground forces to move in and mop up, so the order was finally given to commence the ground war on February 24, 1991.[3]

Despite being about five miles off in the distance, the night skies were brightly illumined with fires caused by the multiple artillery barrages. Smoke filled the air as well.

Kevin and his unit sat expectantly in their position, awaiting the inevitable call to rescue and tend to casualties. Another medical team was first-up, while Kevin's team was second-up.

The fighting was still going strong around two or three in the morning when the order came for the first-up team to launch. The encampment became a flurry of excitement, as they prepared to do their jobs in an actual combat environment. This was what all their training was about.

The other teams looked on with pride as the first-up team quickly performed their pre-flight checks. In a matter of seconds, the aircraft was lifting off the ground. However, something appeared to be going terribly wrong. The aircraft rose as if it were about to climb nose-first in altitude, then it turned and drove nose-first into the ground instead. Only the crew chief survived, though badly burned. Investigators later believed that the night vision goggles had caused the pilots to become disoriented with vertigo, because cloud cover and smoke left them with no stars or moon-light to use as a frame of reference.

The battalion commander directed Kevin's team to launch immediately in the first-up team's place. There was no time for grief as they sprang into action, just as the first-up team had done, and lifted off like routine. With adrenaline pumping, they flew swiftly toward their destination on the horizon. Everyone onboard was truly psyched for the mission awaiting them.

They flew at a very low altitude, called NOE (nap-of-the-earth), to avoid possible detection, while using their night vision goggles to see where they were going. As they drew near to the firefight, they could see the barrel flashes of small arms fire. They radioed ahead for clarification on their destination and got it from the soldier who was calling in the rescue.

When they arrived at the site, Kevin could see enemy tanks not too far away on the horizon. In a glance, however, most of them appeared to be ablaze or smoking.

As the aircraft landed, Kevin hopped out carrying a litter in one hand and his medical aid kit in the other. The crew chief jumped out behind him and began providing cover for the aircraft while Kevin was away. A soldier met Kevin immediately and directed him to follow him to the location of the casualty. In a matter of seconds, they arrived, and Kevin quickly assessed the soldier had a severely wounded leg.

Before Kevin could begin treating the soldier, however, someone screamed,

"INCOMING!"

Kevin instantly spread across his patient to shield him from the shrapnel and other debris that was sure to follow an artillery round's detonation. There was a loud whistling, a thud, and a split second later, there was an enormous explosion.

When the debris settled, Kevin quickly threw the soldier over his back, wrapping one arm around his thigh and grabbing the soldier's wrist with his other hand. Leaving the litter behind, he raced back to the waiting aircraft, where he rolled the man partially inside, while the crew chief dragged him in the rest of the way. Kevin had barely closed the door when someone began shouting,

"Go-Go-Go!"

They lifted off and began the return flight to their encampment. Kevin continued providing medical aid to the soldier's wounded leg and placed it in a stint.

When they arrived back at their base camp, Kevin quickly gave his report on the treatment he had provided and a cursory description of the patient's condition, while the wounded soldier was transferred to the capable care of the waiting medical staff.

Following their return, Kevin and his team had to make preparations for the possibility of additional rescues, though everything became a blur in his memory after that. The one thing he would never forget about that night, however, was that he had watched his fellow medics in the first-up team crash and burn, but he and his team had not even had time to grieve.

The Persian Gulf War would go down as one of the shortest-fought wars in history, lasting only 42 days in total. The majority of that time, 38 days, was allotted to the air war.[4] More than that, though, the public pulled out all the stops in welcoming our troops home after the war, perhaps in an attempt to make up for the appalling way our troops were treated upon their return from the Vietnam War a generation earlier. Kevin and his fellow soldiers returning to Ft. Sill were no exception to this warm welcome.

People lined the interstate and other streets leading from Altus Air Force Base in neighboring Altus, Oklahoma, back to Ft. Sill. They cheered and waved and held "Welcome Home!" signs for all to see. It caused every soldier's heart to swell with pride.

An enormous crowd surrounded the unit area at Ft. Sill when they arrived. A roar of cheers went up as the buses pulled into the Post's airfield parking lot. Family members had evidently been briefed not to interfere with the soldiers as they disembarked and made their way into the hangars.

Inexplicable to anyone, they were marched inside for a series of briefings, to which not one soul paid the least bit of attention. Everyone present knew that waiting just yards away in another hangar were their dear loved ones, impatient to hug and kiss them.

After a fair amount of time, the command of "Fall in!" was finally given to the eager soldiers. Tears began to stream down some of their faces, almost like a Pavlovian response. As soon as the hangar doors opened, the crowd let out another round of cheers, whistles, and applause in anticipation of the soldiers' release. The crowd of onlookers parted like the Red Sea as the soldiers marched toward the other hangar where their families were waiting. The cheering was so loud Kevin and his comrades could barely hear the cadence calls of the First Sergeant as he marched them toward their families.

As they entered the hangar, Kevin heard a familiar voice, even above the din. Cassandra was shouting,

"Zee! Zee!"

He broke military discipline and turned to see her and all his family waving wildly and calling his name. He smiled the broadest smile ever as they made eye contact.

The company commander addressed the formation only briefly before dismissing them to be with their wonderful families. It was mayhem as everyone swarmed together. Kevin had barely turned in the direction of his family when Cassandra leapt into his arms, practically smothering him with hugs and kisses. The rest of his family quickly pressed in on him, hugging and kissing him, too. He looked each one in the eyes and told them how much he loved them and how much he had missed them. The whole experience was far above all he had expected.

The drive home seemed almost unreal. When they arrived, more friends were waiting to share in a welcome home party with him. It was truly heartwarming to have them all there with him.

They had been home only a few minutes, when Cassandra called Kevin to come see their dog, Bruno. They had gotten Bruno, a Chow, as a puppy only a few months before Kevin deployed, and although Cassandra had mailed pictures of him in her letters, Kevin was totally unprepared for what he saw.

As Cassandra whistled and called for Bruno, he came into sight after a few seconds and looked enormous. He had grown so large, and it seemed to Kevin he had been gone a long time, so he feared Bruno would not remember him. Startled by Bruno's size, Kevin quickly closed the door and said,

"Woe! He might not remember me!"

Kevin's reaction caused Cassandra to laugh. She said,

"Of course, he remembers you! Look at him!"

Bruno looked through the sliding glass door with ears perked, smiling his best doggy smile, wagging his tail, and sporting a bright red, white, and blue ribbon over his collar. This looked friendly enough to Kevin, so he decided to risk opening the door and petting Bruno. Bruno tried to lick Kevin's face in a warm greeting. It was as if Kevin had never been gone.

Animal psychologists have said that whether we are gone ten minutes, all day, or longer, it's all the same to dogs. While there may be a limit to dogs' memory, it seemed Bruno had not reached his memory limit during Kevin's deployment, so all was well.

After this, Cassandra urged Kevin to go change into the more comfortable clothes she had laid out on their bed. After months of wearing nothing but desert camouflage, it really felt good to put on some civilian clothes again.

The rest of the party was very relaxed, as Kevin enjoyed renewing acquaintances with his friends and eating something besides Army rations and MREs, for a change. It wasn't long, however, before everyone realized Kevin's tiredness and began to politely retire to their homes. As much fun as it was to have friends and relatives over for a party, it was nice to be alone once again. After some well-deserved block leave, though, it didn't take long to return to routine, albeit, with a few changes.

Over the next year-and-a-half, or more, Kevin continued to perform his daily duties at Ft. Sill. They celebrated their first anniversary a little late, since it occurred during Kevin's deployment, by conducting a small chapel wedding ceremony at the Ft. Sill New Post Chapel that following summer. A family friend, who was an ordained minister, conducted the ceremony for them. Kevin's mother was the only member of their two extended families able to make the trip, but her presence made it truly special for both of them.

The rest of their lives returned to normal, until the inevitable news came of Kevin's next assignment. Kevin was ordered to report to Germany in December 1992. It would prove to be a major source of contention in their family, as reassignments often are for military families. Furthermore, it came at a rather inopportune time for at least one of the children. The oldest was in his first year of college by now, but the next oldest was in his senior year of high school.

Moving in the middle of his senior year was a most unwelcome prospect, so unwelcome, in fact, that he negotiated with Kevin and Cassandra to let him remain in the U. S. with his biological father while they moved to Germany. It was not an easy decision, but ultimately, they allowed it for their son's sake. For Cassandra, it would be one of the most painful decisions and experiences of her life. For Kevin, it would be painful to watch his wife suffer so. In time, however, they managed to move on emotionally, even as they had moved on geo-graphically. Nevertheless, neither of them could have foreseen what would happen next in their lives.

Chapter Six
A Time for Peace

With the glory of Operations Desert Shield and Desert Storm starting to fade behind him, Kevin continued to serve faithfully at Ft. Sill, Oklahoma, until December 1992, when he was reassigned to Landstuhl, Germany. Life in the Army was growing calm and quiet once again, and this next assignment promised to be a nice reward for a lot of hard work.

When Kevin learned he was being reassigned to Germany, he grew excited. This would be his first tour in Europe, and he had a list of historic sites he wanted to visit. With the Cold War effectively ended about a year before Operation Desert Shield began, the Soviet Communist threat was practically nil, and a tour of duty in Germany was now expected to be one of relative ease.

His family was not as excited, however. What had initially been an occasion for celebration had now turned into one of disappointment for Kevin. Nevertheless, they pressed on. With two fewer members of their family than before, life was changing for them in several ways.

Upon arrival and in-processing, the new family of three began to settle in to their new home. Of course, one of the most important decisions they needed to make was where they would attend worship. While worshiping off-post was a sort of given in the United States, it was not so in Germany, where everyone spoke German, except when some of them wanted to practice their English with the Americans living among them.

They soon learned of the Vogelweh Chapel on the installation where Kevin was assigned, so they began attending worship services there. The movement of God upon the services and attendees was apparent, though the chaplain assigned to pastor the congregation appeared to wrestle with a tension between following a more free-flowing style and a more restrained style of worship.

Not long after they began attending worship at Vogelweh, Kevin had to go away on a TDY mission for training. While he was gone, Cassandra attended a Sunday School class conducted by one of the other attendees of the chapel service. The Spiritual anointing with which Lieutenant Colonel John Neal, a comptroller for the installation, led the Bible study made a powerful impact upon Cassandra, so much so that she just had to share it with Kevin when they next spoke by phone. They agreed to continue attending the class together when Kevin returned from his TDY.

Both Kevin and Cassandra grew even more in their spiritual lives under LTC Neal's leadership than they had the previous years at Ft. Sill. Kevin, in particular, became more personally accountable in his daily walk with Christ. Using the Apostle

Paul's analogy in his first letter to the Corinthian Church (3:10-15), they had laid a strong foundation in their worship and fellowship at Ft. Sill, and now in Germany, they were building a magnificent structure out of precious metals and precious stones on that solid foundation. It was truly amazing.

After some time, the tension in the Vogelweh Chapel congregation grew stronger. While LTC Neal never contradicted or undermined the leadership of the chaplain pastor, he finally felt compelled to begin a separate service in which he could worship more freely as he believed. He obtained permission from the senior chaplain leadership to do so, and started the new service in the Landstuhl Chapel soon thereafter. Those in the former service in the Vogelweh Chapel who agreed with LTC Neal's perspective joined him in the new service in the Landstuhl Chapel. Kevin and his family were among those who chose to follow LTC Neal. While it was not an easy decision, they believed the Spiritual anointing upon LTC Neal warranted their continued discipleship under his leadership. The degree of spiritual growth and formation they developed in the ensuing years proved they made the right choice.

Since everything was going so well, there was no way to predict what was about to happen next. Just a few days short of exactly two years after arriving in Landstuhl, Germany, Kevin and his unit headed into a new hot spot in the world — Bosnia. Rumors had been circulating that the U. S. would get involved in the ethnic conflict flaring up there after decades of peace, but Kevin did not even suspect that his unit would be called into action on account of it. Once again, he found himself saying goodbye to his dear family just before one of the most important holidays of the year – Christmas. It was déjà vu all over again!

It was not quite the same as the Persian Gulf War, but it was not exactly a walk in the park either. Although it was technically a peace-keeping mission, the potential for harm was still prevalent. The stroll through that minefield along the unpaved road was just such evidence of the danger that existed all around them. In fact, it was that very event which had stirred all this reminiscing in the first place and which has led us back full-circle to this point in our story.

Kevin had no idea how long he had been daydreaming about how far he had come in his life, but he finally came back to reality and considered how blessed of God he truly was. He thanked God then and there for all his many blessings. It was something he would never forget.

As time marched on for Kevin and his unit, they continued to perform their medical duties alongside their Norwegian counterparts. Although none of them had forgotten the miraculous way in which they had rescued and tended the Swiss casualties that day, life being how it is, they had pushed it to the back of their minds now to make room for current events. Just as they had never expected to witness such a miracle on their previous mission, however, they had no expectation of ever witnessing something like it again. Perhaps that is precisely why God chose to reveal His power in such a way once more.

It was late-afternoon, but still daylight, on April 4, 1996. Once again, it was raining steadily, though it was not nearly as cold by this time of the year. Kevin and his comrades had grown accustomed to conducting missions involving landmines, but none of them compared to that previous miraculous encounter he had had back in January, shortly after his arrival. That is, until now.

Suddenly, the loudspeaker blared again, "MEDEVAC! MEDEVAC! MEDEVAC!"

Everyone sprang into action, each performing his function that made the mission succeed time and again. CW2 Dave White was the IC for Kevin's team. Although Kevin's team s second-up, they were called to action, to t the front desk, just before his departure, Kevin learned why when he heard the words,

"Two soldiers down in the Russian Brigade. Both are lying in what is safe to assume is a heavily-infested mine field."

Kevin's blood ran cold. "Oh, God!" he prayed under his breath. "Please don't let this be happening again! God, *please*!"

Kevin tried to conceal his fear and deep reservations about taking on this mission. His mind raced in tandem with his pulse as he contemplated the danger and risk before him once again. He just kept praying silently, "Lord, please, don't let this be happening again!"

As they launched and flew toward the scene, more details came to them over the radio. The two soldiers had walked some distance away from their camp when one stepped on a land mine. The second tried to go for help, but he got only 35-50 meters before he also stepped on a mine. Kevin's prayerful petition would not be granted this time.

When they arrived at the scene of the incident, the first-up pilot landed approximately one-quarter mile away from the site. CW2 White thought that would be too far to walk, however, especially when transporting the casualty back to the aircraft, so he found a spot a little closer to the site.

In fair weather, the pilot would fly over the area a couple of times to insure there were no anti-tank mines visible. Anti-tank mines could be spotted by the short tilt rod that extended upward about 12 inches from the mine, and with as little as 2.9 pounds of pressure (easily exceeded by a helicopter's rotor wash), they would be detonated. (In retrospect, Kevin firmly believed it was an anti-tank mine that had detonated and caused so much damage on his earlier mission in January.) Next, the pilot would hover long enough to lower the medic with a litter, and fly off until recalled. Then he would return to hoist them back into the aircraft for the return flight to the hospital. Due to the rain today, however, that would not be feasible.

Once on the ground, Kevin picked his way carefully toward the scene of the injured. He felt numb all over as he struggled to keep his fear in check.

He had gone only about ten yards when his heart practically stopped at what he saw. He had just stepped less than two inches to the side of a land mine. It was made partially visible by the rain. All he could do was stare at it, while both his heart and his mind were racing wildly. It must have been the Spirit of God Who nudged him to continue his trek ahead toward the wounded soldier. It was certainly God Who helped him keep his focus on the mission of treating the wounded soldier rather than upon his own trepidation. He resumed his step and soon came to where the two soldiers lay.

The other medic had arrived from his march just as Kevin did. Since one of the soldiers lay near the other medic, he chose to treat that one, and Kevin took the second.

As Kevin finished treating the casualty, other soldiers had gathered around to watch from what they believed to be the perimeter of the mine field. He solicited the help of two of them, and with the crew chief from his aircraft, they began to pick their way back toward the waiting helicopter. Each took his turn pointing out what he believed to be a land mine, as they slowly and painstakingly made their way back to safety.

The safest place to land the helicopter had turned out to be on a nearby slope, which made it more dangerous to re-embark, because the main rotor blades were much closer to the ground on the uphill side in that case. Perhaps that feat was a lot easier to deal with than side-stepping the dangers of a mine field, however.

Kevin heaved a great sigh of relief as they took off for the return flight to the hospital. He continued to monitor the wounded soldier's condition as they flew.

When they arrived, he quickly updated the nurse on the treatment he had provided and on the patient's condition before handing the patient over to the medical team's care. All this was done in a matter of seconds, as they whisked the patient off for further treatment.

Once back at his unit headquarters, Kevin was debriefed by the command, and then released to go unwind. He headed for his room, but he felt he needed to share his story with someone. He sought out his good friend, Joe Sands, since Joe had been present for the previous miracle in January. Surely, Joe would understand better than anyone else what he had just experienced. Another fellow medic was also present as Kevin told his story. After a moment of solemn reflection, while the whole realization sank into their minds, they all gave praise to God for once again performing a miracle that had spared Kevin's life.

Witnessing just one such miracle would have been sufficient to change anyone's mind about

God's constant supervision in our lives, but to witness *two* such miracles compelled Kevin to ask, "Why?"

Why had God selected *him* to be the recipient of these two miracles? What did God want him to do with these two experiences?

Kevin's mind wandered off into deeper contemplation as he considered how God had been so good to him throughout his life. At that time, his humility would not even allow him to consider the prospect of sharing his story in print. He did not know how God would use his story, but he was convinced God had a holy purpose in it. He filed the whole thing away in his memory for later, eventual retrieval when the time was right. There was no way he could have foreseen what God would do next to facilitate this endeavor.

Chapter Seven
A Time to Speak

Kevin returned to Germany from Bosnia at the end of 1996. It had been another difficult time of coping with separation from his family, but once again, it was now in the past. Looking back on such ordeals is always easier than looking ahead. Even enduring them is easier than anticipating them, because focusing on the mission at hand is the best way to distract oneself from the painful loneliness of separation. Nevertheless, somewhat like the pangs of childbirth (see John 16:21), deployment is soon forgotten amidst the joys of reunion and the return to routine.

Kevin spent another eighteen months completing his tour of duty in Germany before being assigned to his next duty station: Ft. Lewis, Washington. That would prove to be his final assignment before retirement in January 2001.

Before retiring from the Army, Kevin would receive two more honors for his selfless heroism, besides the miracles we have already spotlighted in this book. He would be nominated for and awarded not one, but *two* Soldier's Medals, something only a rare few have ever been honored to receive.

The Soldier's Medal is awarded to those who risk their lives to perform some kind of selfless, heroic act to save another's life other than in combat. Both of the times Kevin faced down danger to his own life to save another's in those mine fields certainly qualified for these awards. He received the first award in December 1998, and he received the second in January 2000.

Not being one to seek the spotlight, all this attention made Kevin uncomfortable. However, God was preparing him to cast a bigger net to capture a wider audience. Putting his story into a book would help many more people to understand the miraculous power of God in his life. Perhaps some of them would finally identify and acknowledge the miracles God had wrought in their own lives and choose to draw nearer to God as a result.

Having worked in a medical profession for 20 years, Kevin was ready for an occupational change. In the first several months following retirement from the Army, he worked for a corporation in Human Resources. This corporate job, though satisfying, was cut short by a layoff after only one year following the 9-11 attacks. He found another job in the same line of work in a hospital, but this turned out to be a poor match, since the corporate politics there proved rather brutal. He spent the next 16 months accepting work through a temporary job agency. Despite its being considered part-time, God nonetheless kept Kevin employed full-time all but two weeks during those 16 months.

It was also during this first year or so following Kevin's retirement from the Army that he happened to watch a program on television that questioned why miracles do not happen today as they did in Bible times. He immediately thought of the two miracles God had wrought in his own life in Bosnia. Despite his modesty about his heroics, he couldn't get out of his mind the idea now that God wanted him to tell his miraculous story as an encouragement to others.

Feeling inadequate to the task of writing it himself, he began searching for someone else to write it for him. After approximately one year of fruitless searching, Kevin was referred by some people in his local area to the FaithWriters.com web site for help.

Faith Writers is a web-based, Christian organization focused on helping would-be Christian writers and professionals alike to find work and get expert help for their writing skill. The organization seeks to connect writers with publishers and publishers with writers. The web site contains helpful articles on writing and publishing, a plethora of forums for sharing writing and marketing tips, opportunities to showcase their writings to potential publishers looking for content, and much more. They offer both free and paid subscription services. They truly are a blessing to Christian writers.

After Kevin contacted the good folks at Faith Writers with his request for help, they sent out a private message to everyone on their Private Messenger subscription service asking for anyone interested in writing the book for Kevin to email him. A good number of respondents made contact, but when Kevin read my response, he felt he had found the one God intended to write this story. After a few email exchanges, he was certain I was to be the one.

Kevin says it was my previous writing experience coupled with my military experience that convinced him to choose me. I believe it was the Spirit of God Who chose to put us both together in carrying out this mission of glorious hope.

However you choose to see it, I hope you have been truly blessed by Kevin's story and that because of it, you can now see where God has wrought some wonderful miracles in your own life. Maybe you can recall a near-accident when you were spared a certain death. Perhaps you remember a time when you or someone you love dearly was facing a life-threatening illness that was miraculously cured after a time of prayer. Could it be that God is prompting you to share your personal story of victory with the world? It certainly is worth considering.

Our Lord truly is a wonderful God, and thanks to the faithfulness of a godly man like Kevin Zimmerman, who obeyed the Lord's urging to share his personal story with us, we now see the glory of our Lord in a way that perhaps we had not considered before. God surely is still in the miracle-working business in our own day and time. Praise the Lord, and blessed be the name of our God!

Epilogue

Much has happened since I began this writing project. When I accepted the task, I expected I would be able to accomplish it in a short time and move on to the next project. However, what I thought would have taken only a few weeks to a few months to write actually took me over two and one-half years to complete!

First, there was the distressing prospect of having to leave the active Army, which I did, in fact, at the end of 2005. During those waning months while waiting to learn where I would be employed as a minister, I found it impossible to concentrate on anything other than where I was going next and how I would provide for my family.

Next, after I left the active Army, I joined a part-time Army Reserve unit in Dothan, Alabama, where I thought I would live and work after I left the Army. However, God had other plans for me, so I accepted a full-time pastoral position with a small membership church west of Mobile, Alabama. I found myself confronted with all the usual pastoral duties, plus the responsibility of resettling my family into our first-ever, personally owned home. I have also since transferred into the Alabama Army National Guard in order to perform my monthly military duties closer to where I live, and I finally received that much-desired promotion to Major. To top all this, God quite unexpectedly moved me yet again to a new congregation a short distance from Mobile, which turned out to be my happiest location ever in serving Him. However, I left there at the end of 2011 in order to pursue a new direction in pastoral ministry which is turning out to be a grand adventure with Christ.

As life began to calm down a bit for me after I left the Army at the end of 2005, I gradually regained my initial enthusiasm and inspiration for writing this story. In the spring of 2006, I began writing more in earnest. As I said earlier in this book, I felt compelled of God to complete it.

Around that same time (April 2006), I established my own Christian independent publishing house, Parson Place Press, partly to have a means of publishing this book, and partly to have a means of publishing other future works. You can read more about this endeavor and check out other inspiring titles at www.parsonplacepress.com.

We were finally able to release the first edition of this book for public sale and distribution in May 2008, but after more than three years in circulation, I thought it would be good to update it with what has happened in Kevin's life since 2008 by releasing a revised second edition. You are reading the result of that update now.

Though there have been many distractions from the writing of this book, God has remained faithful with inspiring me and has enabled me to complete it in His Own good time. Through it all, I have been continually amazed at Kevin's understanding and patience with me. Had our roles been reversed, I am not so sure I would have measured up to his standard. Next to God's faithfulness, I am *most* grateful for Kevin's patient and godly encouragement. May God reward him one hundred fold!

Here we are, at last, at the end of our journey. I pray Kevin's story has touched your heart and life as much as it has mine. Truly, his story harmonizes with our own. There really is a time for everything.

To find out more about where Kevin is now and what he has been doing since his retirement from the Army, read the personal update following this chapter. You can contact him at the address he has provided there, too, in case you want to send him well wishes, etc.

A Personal Update on Kevin Zimmerman

After retiring from the Army, Kevin first settled in the Dallas, Texas, area where he lived until 2010. Since the publication of the first edition of this book in 2008, Kevin has experienced a number of changes in his life. In order to lay them out a little more clearly, he has divided them into calendar years, beginning with 2008, when the first edition was published. These events are as follows in Kevin's own words.

2008: This was a very challenging year. The real estate industry collapsed, dramatically impacting our business. Home sales decreased and home owner's property insurance began to fall off the books due to foreclosure.

2009: I took on a position in 2009 with a Law Firm that specialized in Tax law. Over time, I had become the Senior Manager in the client services department. Nevertheless, due to a declining economy, the company began to feel the effects. I witnessed the company grow to approximately 126 employees in 2009 to encountering gradual layoffs. Being engaged to Mary Ann (Mari), I found myself constantly resisting anxiety as she and Tiffany, my daughter, legitimately questioned the stability of the company.

2010: Their concerns finally became a reality just before Mari and I took our yearly trip to Massachusetts for the holidays in December of 2010. Prior to departing, it was expressed at the firm that we thought we were on pace and no one else had to lose their job. On November 30, 2010, I was notified by a member in my department that she had been laid off. Upon contacting my peers, I discovered more disturbing news. The company had down-sized to approximately 20 to 30 people. Another thing became clear. With no people, who was I going to manage? The entire department was laid off. I had gone from an entry position, to Senior Manager, now back to being grateful I had a job. I no longer enjoyed showing up every day. One week later, I received a message from one of my previous Lieutenant Colonels. I served as his Operations NCOIC on my last assignment prior to retirement from the U. S. Army. He was sharing that he was in San Antonio and wanted to touch base. I had been very sick that week and did not reply. The next day, another message was left, this time emphasizing the importance of contacting him. I gathered enough strength and made the call.

I was offered the position of Deputy Program Manager of Operations (DPMO) for the ANAM Program (Automated Neuropsychological Assessment Metrics)[5]. The program's home office was relocating from Alexandria, Virginia, to San

Antonio, Texas, leaving a vacancy in the DPMO position. The program falls under the Army's TBI (Traumatic Brain Injury) program and is a computer generated test that captures short term memory and basic cognitive function. The position required relocating to San Antonio, Texas, yet the package was justifiable. My concern was Mari. She had made the decision to leave everyone and everything she knew in Massachusetts to join me in McKinney, Texas. I knew she loved living in McKinney as much as the Dallas-McKinney area. With our intent to marry, along with considering her personal sacrifice, I knew I could not provide an answer without considering her opinion. Yet, when I explained our circumstances, she provided total support.

2011: In February of 2011, I accepted the position, and in April, we moved to San Antonio. The miracle of this situation is that my Lieutenant Colonel and I had not communicated since my retirement in January of 2000. With a declining economy and a company down-size, God spanned 11 years and chose me to serve the soldier again, this time with a lot less stress and a lot more pay.

I'm now consistently learning the requirements of the new position and promoting this book throughout the region. Mari is also working on enhancing her gift as an Interior Designer. She has already begun building her clientele. We have found a great place to worship, are enjoying the blessings of God, and are having fun planning our wedding.

Truly, God has blessed Kevin far beyond all that he could ask or imagine (Ephesians 3:20). All glory and honor and praise be unto God now and forever! Amen!

As one final thank you, Kevin wishes to add: "I would like to thank all of my family, relatives and friends who supported me on this project. I give special thanks to Tiffany, Maryann (Mari), and Niesha, three very special women whose motivational support provided the inspiration to complete what I had started. Also, to Tyrone and Anthony, my irons which sharpen iron, who, for the entire initial three year effort, never ceased to provide many words of encouragement that this day would surely come."

If you wish to contact Kevin to thank him for sharing his story or just to swap "war stories," you can email him at: atfekz@gmail.com at any time. He welcomes your feedback.

Appendix A
Glossary of Terms

AIT – Advanced Initial Training; the job skill training every initial entry trainee (IET) soldier receives after finishing basic combat training.

APC – Armored Personnel Carrier; a small, track vehicle used to transport small squads of soldiers.

ASVAB – Armed Services Vocational Aptitude Battery; a qualifying test everyone must pass before being accepted for U. S. military service.

BCT – Basic Combat Training; the initial, basic war-fighting training every soldier receives when s/he first enlists in the Army.

Cantonment – The Main Post environment where soldiers live, work, and conduct their day-to-day activities.

Chain of Command – the hierarchy of leadership segmented at each level within the Army.

CO – Commissioned Officer; can also sometimes mean Commanding Officer.

Crew Chief – an enlisted soldier who assists the pilot(s) with take-off and landing preparations, with defensive measures, with minor maintenance and repairs of the aircraft, and with passenger accommodations aboard the aircraft.

CW2 – Chief Warrant Officer, Second Grade; a junior level rank among warrant officers in the Army. Most warrant officers in the Army follow one of three channels: technical, supply, or aircraft pilot.

DFAC – Dining Facility (pronounced Dee-Fack), also sometimes called the mess hall or chow hall by "old timers".

Drill and Ceremony – also called D & C, it is the marching of troops, and the specific commands which direct them.

1SG – First Sergeant (pay grade E-8); a senior level enlisted rank in the Army.

FTX – Field Training Exercise; a training event conducted in the outdoors, usually well removed from outside interference.

General Discharge – one of four types of discharge from the U. S. armed forces; in order of best to worst, they are Honorable, General, Bad Conduct, and Dishonorable. Any discharge other than honorable is completely undesirable.

LTC – Lieutenant Colonel (pay grade O-5); a mid-level, senior officer rank in the Army.

MEDEVAC – Medical Evacuation, as in medevac helicopter or ambulance.

MRE – Meal, Ready to Eat; a shelf-stable ration of food that soldiers eat when hot meals are unavailable.

NCO – Noncommissioned Officer, "the backbone of the Army".

NCOIC – Noncommissioned Officer in Charge (an NCO appointed over a group of Soldiers, a special project, a building, or any number of other areas of responsibility).

NOE – Nap-of-the-earth; when an aircraft flies as close to the earth as possible to avoid radar detection.

PFC – Private First Class (pay grade E-3); a lower enlisted rank in the Army.

PIC – Pilot in Command; the senior pilot aboard an aircraft.

Platoon – a group of three-to-five squads.

Platoon Guide – a junior enlisted soldier, usually in basic combat training, who is charged with being a liaison between the platoon and the chain of command.

PVT – Private (pay grade E-1); the lowest enlisted rank in the Army.

PX – Post Exchange; the Main PX is the department store on Post where practically everything from post cards to music CDs to snack foods to hardware can be purchased. Branch PXs, often called shoppettes, are usually much smaller and are more like convenience stores.

SGT – Sergeant (pay grade E 5); a junior noncommissioned officer rank in the Army.

SPC – Specialist (pay grade E-4); a junior enlisted soldier rank in the Army. Many years ago, the Army used to have Specialist ranks E-4 through E-6, but the SP5 and SP6 ranks were phased out sometime during the 1980s, and the SP4 rank was renamed as SPC.

SSG – Staff Sergeant (pay grade E-6); a mid-level noncommissioned officer rank in the Army.

TDY – Temporary Duty; a special orders duty status for soldiers who are attending specialized training, encompassing everything from military schooling to civilian teaching conferences.

U. N. – United Nations; a world organization comprised of member nations from all around the globe for the purpose of addressing social and political issues throughout the world.

End Notes

1. In the first edition, I mistakenly wrote that I left the Army as a Private First Class, but that is actually the rank at which I first entered the Army in 1981. I actually left the Army at the rank of Specialist (E-4) in 1984. I apologize for this confusion.

2. http://www.rand.org/pubs/monograph_ reports/MR775/MR775.chap5.pdf, p.63

3. Ibid.

4. Ibid.

5. http://www.armymedicine.army.mil/prr/ anam.html

Other Titles
from Parson Place Press
For more information regarding discounts, see
www.parsonplacepress.com/store

Digital Evangelism: You Can Do It, Too!
By Michael L. White
ISBN 13: 978-0-9842163-2-1

Add digital evangelism to your repertoire of
ministry skill

From Slave to Governor: the Unlikely Life of Lott Cary
By Perry Thomas
ISBN 13: 978-0-9786567-9-9

A tribute to God's amazing grace

The Unseen War: Winning the Fight for Life
by David K. Kortje
ISBN 13: 978-0-9786567-7-5

Spiritual warfare may be one of the most
significant aspects of the Christian life.

Good News from Indonesia: Heartwarming Stories from the Land of the Tsunami
by Perry Thomas
ISBN 13: 978-0- 9842163-4-5

Your vicarious missionary experience begins
here

Other Titles
from Parson Place Press

For more information regarding discounts, see
www.parsonplacepress.com/store

The Robins of St. Lawrence Church

Story and Full-color Illustrations by Amy Dyas
ISBN 13: 978-0-9786567-8-2

Take off on this high-flying adventure

Seasons of the Heart

by Lori Stratton
ISBN 13: 978-0-9786567-2-0

Let your heart be stirred anew

Louisa

by Richard Emmel
ISBN 13: 978-0-9786567-3-7

Based on the life of American poet, Phillis
Wheatley

The Resource Book for Louisa: A Guide for Teachers

by Gena McReynolds and Richard Emmel
ISBN 13: 978-0-9786567-5-1

For elementary and middle school teachers

CPSIA information can be obtained at www.ICGtesting.com
Printed in the USA
LVOW130008210512

282436LV00001BA/11/P